A Voyage In My Self

3 months on the Indian road, in poetry

Including the
2nd Edition of
Tasting The Spring
Where Pictures Sing

Kevan Myers

June to September
2006

Published by CompletelyNovel, 2020,
for
Dancing Yeti Books.

Copyright © Kevan Myers 2006 & 2020

Kevan Myers has asserted his right under the Copyright, Designs and Patents Act 1988 to be identified as the author of this work.

Cover art: from Collage Of A Road in Tiruvannamalai by Harriet Lissauer, in a cover designed by Kevan Myers, helped by Sanjay Beery & Karen Peck. All yetis by D.R.Postgate

This book is sold subject to the condition that it shall not, by way of trade or otherwise, be lent, resold, hired out, or otherwise circulated without the publisher's prior consent in any form of binding or cover other than that in which it is published and without a similar condition including this condition being imposed on the subsequent purchaser

ISBN 9781787234789

Facebook page:
'Kevan Myers: poems and thoughts': http://bit.ly/2JQETk1

Website: kevanmyerspoetry.com

Preface To The 2nd Edition
(with some words on its new title)

The first edition of this book was completed in 2006.

All through its editing and preparation, I worked with the title **'A Voyage In My Self'**, which I loved because it seemed so apt. But someone persuaded me that it was not suitable, and I cannot remember why, but I dropped it and replaced it with the title: **'Tasting The Spring Where Pictures Sing'**, and it never felt quite right.

Now this is my 2nd edition, retaining much from the first, but also encompassing many changes and so I've switched back to my original working title

When meeting a new poetry book, many readers open it randomly and jump from page to page, so the author may hope that if some poems cause yawns or anguish, the next jump may change the mood.

But this book has proved different, as those who bought the first edition often told me they liked it because the poems could be read as a journey from beginning to end, which naturally tugged them out of any dull or difficult bits, but I hope I have now erased them.

I'm my own editor, and hard to satisfy. As soon as a work is printed, I start to find things I want to improve. After the typos, I work on the language, rhythms and lack of clarity. So I've cut some poems, rewritten others, and added three, which I started with the rest of the poems in this book, but didn't finish in time for the first edition. I've also added a short **Part II**, with poems that I wrote at different times on other Indian journeys, for a bit of contrast in matter and style.

Finally, I hope that now you've climbed aboard for the voyage,, the experience will be worth every penny you've paid for the ticket.

Contents

Preface To The 2nd Edition
Dedication
Foreword

Part I: A Voyage In Myself

Letters For An Empty Page	1
Learning To Say Goodbye	2
Exiled Faces From High Places	4
The Cost Of Living	6
Chacun à Son Goût	6
Best Of Friends	7
Keeping Sight Bright	7
Amaizing Grace	7
Unsolved Philosophical Question	8
Between Two Words	8
Ani (Tibetan Nun)	8
Compassion	9
Before The Lens	10
Observing The Obvious	11
Lifetime Search	11
Some Winds Do Not Pass	11
Now I Find Out Why	12
Here I Raise My Hat	12
Going Walkies	12
Exiles Who've Never Left Home	13
Lofty Amputations	14
Haiku, [Plus Optional Words]	14
Zoological Observation	14
Rainy Weather	15
Sartorial Discomfort	15
Side Effects of Religion	15
Indian Decibels	16
Paradoxes Transcend Time	16
Invisible Blues	16
Where The Eyes May Lie	17
Problem Of Startling Dimensions	17
Inner Secret Of Buffoon	18
How Snaps Can Crackle And Pop	18
Still Trying To Figure It Out	19
Riding Away From The Vultures' Café	19

The Body I Cannot Control	20
The Pleasure Of Not Turning Back	21
Rise & Shine	22
A True Reward For Public Service	22
Flickers Of The Past	21
Words That Are Hard To Say	23
Words That Grow Easier To Say	24
Full House	25
Eyeing The Forbidden Fruit	26
Helping Me On "The Way"	27
Something To Chuang Tzu On	27
The Gourmet's Treat	28
Neighbours Not Chosen, But Planted	28
Looking About	29
Exactly Where Do I Find My Ear?	29
Foggy Morning Meditation	30
Holy Grail	32
Catch 21.9	32
Making Mean Faces	33
Malignant Humours	34
Suspect Presents From The Present	34
On Losing Choosing	34
The Joy Of Counselling Couples	35
Chucking Down The Gauntlet	35
To One, Whose Words Speak More Than Their Sum	36
On Those Who Disgrace Their Race	37
Etiquette Cannot Be Taught To Thought	37
Postcard Piece	38
Choosing The Cards To Discard	39
Giving Away The Piggy-Bank	39
Tossing The Coin With No Sides	40
Pedigree Chum	40
Crystal Balls Are Misty	41
Blessings On Their Perceptive Minds	41
The Value Of Contrast	42
Red-Faced Sahib Ungrunts	42
Two Poems on the Effects of Catharsis on Arses	43
When Skies Descend	43

Nainital	44
Dawn	48
With No Specks On My Specs	48
Looking Back Before I'm Gone	49
Visionary Substance	50
On Not Discussing Where To Put The Change	51
Afterthought On Recent Lines	51
Just Call Me Tate, Mate	52
Hearing When You're Not Here	52
Real Friends Have No Ends	53
The Clock's Alarm Cannot Harm	54
The Sound of Two Ears Waggling	55
What Is Before And After	55
How The Future Becomes Present	56
The Point Of The Book	56
The End Of The Road	57

Part II: Some Moments From Different Indian Yoyages

Silent Night, Holy Night	58
Indian Child	59
Song From A Minaret	59
Holy Neighbours	60
What Is Masochism?	60
Seecret Rendezvous	60
On The Swami;s Birthday	61
Drought	62
Thirst	62
Skyholed	62
Poem In Two Movements	63
Attempting Non-Discrimination	64
On trying To Stretch A moment	65
Roadside View	66
Benares	66
Ganga	66
About The Author	68

Dedication

I dedicate these words to those who have helped me to see what is always right here and cannot be lost.

There are many of them, and it's impossible to list every moment, stone and tree, as well as all those friends, whose beings will always be a part of me; but when I was travelling and writing these words, those who touched me closely were the late Radha Ma, whose love and presence gave me safety in places where accidents happen; Karl Renz and Mooji, who helped me awaken to these moments when the outside is in, and Adyashanti, whose words would sometimes make my ears alive as my eyes.

There were also the people of India: always present and observing from somewhere; curious, well-intentioned and kind, often incredibly maddening, noisy and unwilling to allow me peace, and thus the greatest kickers of complacency for anyone, who thinks they've made it and their journey's done.

Amongst them are some of the most frightening, insensitive, stupid and brilliant drivers in the World, who ensured that I had to be very awake to survive. And that helped keep the cobwebs from my mind when I picked up my pen.

So, many thanks to one and all.

Foreword

These poems record my inner and outer discoveries, during the three months which followed the theft of my laptop computer; as I learned again the joy of writing with a pen, which arrived with the greatest rush of poetry that I've met in my life.

For much of this time I had few external pre-occupations as I made the 5,000 km return leg of a long motor-bike ride, along the Himalayan roads from Dharmsala to Badrinath, and then via Kumaon and Lucknow back to my home, near Tiruvannamalai, at the foot of its holy mountain, deep in the South of India.

Many of these poems emerged in a style I have barely touched on before: short, epigrammatic, and dependent on rhymes which are so simple they often verge on the banal. This is partly because writing with pen and paper forces an economy that comes to the point much faster than my work on a laptop, where words and ideas can be moved about before they fly away, or get lost in illegible scrawl..

Since returning I have indeed put this computer process to work, and it has improved some of the longer works, but the shorter ones remain relatively untouched, since much of their editing had already been done, in longhand, during my trip. I've also added a few new ones where spaces demanded some special lines, or earlier words seemed to call for a response.

In previous collections, I have grouped my poems together by themes, taking little account of the gaps in years that separated their times of creation; but these poems must stand in a book by themselves because they are so different from my past work; and because they were written on a journey that I travelled as much within my self as on the roads I took,
I have decided to present them in much the same order in which they came, which allows the inner and outer scenery that I have recorded to reflect, face to face, and thus the reader may see them as part of a developing story, that sometimes slides two steps down as I try to walk up one.

There are poems here which I hope will survive my death, and others which are likely to be quickly forgotten, because they are not profound, or because they record my reactions to passing political events.

Though many are short, I often find them more satisfying than the longer poems which have more room to stray into connecting lines which may lack the fire and originality which should always be present in poetry. These shorter poems are also easier to remember and revisit, and I hope you will. But, whatever their length, many of them attempt to put in words the inexpressible reality, which is always right now.

The ideas in these poems, now seem common-sense to me because I am used to them. Though for much of my life they would have seemed interesting, but strange. So in case you find yourself as bewildered, as I would have been, I'll explain a bit about "**advaita**", which means **'non-duality'**, in Sanskrit.

This experience tells me that the awareness, which appears to be myself, cannot be separated from the other input from the senses and the thoughts. Thus the thought that says "I am a being, separate from all others," is just one among many other thoughts that pass by. For, in truth, this separate being has never been found and therefore remains no more specially myself than this transient scene I see and the sounds of distant cars and birds that I hear. Thus these poems are just saying again and again that everything I experience is as much my Self as this body and this collection of moving thoughts to which my parents gave the name which I still use.

Behind, before, and beyond all experience, unbound by space and time, this Self is here, so all-encompassing and paradoxical, that no words can describe it.

The poems in this book don't stand a chance, however hard they try. Only the spaces between them can be trusted to never lie.

Letters For An Empty Page

I have to put a poem here
because a book begins
with emptiness and words
laid face to face

But even on this wordy side
these letters are no more than lines
contorted in strange postures
like a yoga class
of adepts, dressed in black,
spread out in lines
across an empty place.

They mark the path
that souls might make,
if dipped in ink,
before they fly through space,
or sink without a trace,
between these lines that mark
the boundaries they think.

So hopefully your eyes
may find some meaning
in these signs
on which they lie
as briefly as these moments
live and die.

October 2006, Tiruvannamalai

McCleod Ganj   20th June 2006

Learning To Say Goodbye

The other day
I stole my laptop from myself.
I don't know why I did it, or
the reason that I wore
the blond-streaked hair
and trendy gear
of some Tibetan,
teenage dope-head,
as my own disguise.

Why did I do it?
Do I need this test
of my reactions
to this kind of stress?

Why, when I found
the broken lock
and empty desk,
was I so calm,
when other times
would have me wail
and beat my breast?

Was it because I knew
the hand that carried out this crime
was just as truly mine
as this, which writes these words,
or that, which grabs my arm,
and whines, "baksheesh!",
which makes this other hand of mine
let go its pen and form a fist,
to threaten this intruder
who has barged into its bliss?

My much beloved, expensive tool is gone,
and though I miss its music
and the satsangs* I would hear each day,
its pages of my poetry, its games,
and photos of my family and friends,

I do not think that anything is gone
I cannot live without,
and anything that matters
can be found somewhere
inside my mind,
if need is there.

And thus I carry on,
waiting to see the consequence and why,
I should have removed this precious toy
 from I.

Yet still I must confess
to feeling vexed and insecure,
not knowing when
I'll come back next
to steal more.

*"Satsang" is Sanskrit for "meeting in truth", which hopefully
happens when seekers and spiritual teachers get together.

Exiled Faces From High Places

Flowers crowd and climb
out of their pots,
so full of earth that this veranda
staggers on its feet
and cracks the plaster on the walls,
like whorls in fingerprints that speak
of lives unique;
or like the paint that's grown old,
on portraits, unrestored,
that honestly record
the deep experience and strife
of those, who stand outside their land,
in exile for life.

Their flesh is etched with lines,
like hachured maps
which speak the hardships
of their journey, which
now takes a break
on these smooth stones,
which bear their bones,
where they are sat
to knit and chat,
on each side of their door,
which I must pass
as I go up and down
the rocky path that leads to town.

And thus it is, that long before
I find them there, I start to shed
the rubbish that conceals my soul
in hope to make it fit to meet
the love, so deep,

that's written on their faces
each time I draw near,
as if they're only waiting to embrace
some long-lost grandson,
never met before.

Is it because they see in me
some special joy or grace?
I hope this is the case.
But every friend I meet
who walks this path,
and knows this special pair
has met the same
unspoken peace,
so radiantly here
that as they pass this place,
all hardness seems to melt
inside the sinews of their face.

For in this silent meeting,
love creates a mirror of itself,
that anyone can share,
without a space to intervene:
for none is there.

The path, by their door, wound its way up to McCleod Ganj from my room in the village of Dasalni, with its veranda, where I'd love to sit, often with Nonna, my neighbour, sharing the view of the villagers' fields, that dropped in terraces, down to the valley below.

They wore a scattering of trees, so carelessly rooting themselves, they somehow fell in places that no landscaper could possibly arrange so well.

Around their trunks, the two-cow ploughs were dragged, and then, with speed, almost miraculous, the seed that was thrown became bright green shoots and the stalks and leaves of the maize plants shot upwards with a powerful burst of life.

They seemed to have voices, so full of natural exuberance that my poems must record some of the chats we shared:

The Cost Of Living

The yoga man charges 100 a session,
the masseuse: 500, or more,
but this field of maize,
with its scattered trees,
will answer all your needs
each time you stick your head
outside the door.

Chacun à Son Goût*

Under my veranda,
water, wild with rains, and full
of overflow from loos and drains,
conveys some dreadful stinks,
but in the field below
the maize gets high
from all the shit it drinks.

*Each one to their own taste

Best Of Friends

Sitting beside me on the terrace,
Nonna, with her clown face,
making itself smile.

Keeping Sight Bright

To raise up hope is not a good idea
where life may drop me deeper in despair,
but as I peer between these bars,
through which may come the light,
I have to hope that hope might just be right.

Amaizing Grace

With so much rain to drink,
the juicy green stalks of the maize grow high
and peer up at my feet
from their terrace, below where I
look down from mine.
"Hi, what are you doing up there?" they say.
"Oh, just watching my grief and sickness
flowing
away."

Unsolved Philosophical Question

The maize seems very happy
now the rains have come,
but can its silky hair
go blond without the sun?

Between Two Words

'Illusion' and 'truth' are only words,
but this must be the real thing,
because there are no words
to wrap it in.

'Ani'
(Tibetan Nun)

Surprised,
in the bazaar,
I find
an 'ani',
with eyes
so wide-open
they seem
to be blind.

Compassion

Grunting upwards, lazy legs,
unused to mountain paths,
weighed double by my bag,
and short of gasping breath,
I step aside, to let the faster feet
of this Tibetan girl go past.

But she, instead, stops by my side,
and smiling, takes in hand
one handle from my bag
and slows her stride
to match my pace.

And so we walk up
hand by hand,
with me, inadequate to speak
the thanks I feel,
but most of all,
the joy that there can be
in this humility
which puts me in my place,
just meeting with this sister
from the human race.

Before The Lens

The pictures that no lens could take
are those that shake this emptiness
into the shape, that I
believe is me.

The impact of this art is such
it often leaves my heart outside,
where every touch
may be the reason why
I make this choice to live and die.

Compared to this quite normal state
the snaps we take seem very bland,
and these few moments they collect
from some desire to resurrect
some moment, long time dead,
have no more substance
than the oil poured on waves,
which has the cheek,
to slap cheap make-up
on a face, impossible to grasp,
and countless fathoms deep.

Observing the Obvious

The beauty which surrounds me
is not mine.
And yet, without my eyes to see
it could not be,
and so I guess it comes from me,
and that is fine.

Lifetime Search

The ugliness that I perceive
I'd rather leave behind,
so tell me please where I can find
a dump to leave my mind.

Some Winds Do Not Pass

Will earth spit out our trash?
No, it just seems to eat, and wipe its lips.
Why then do we feel such fear?

Is it the pain and the gas
in its guts we hear?

Now I Find Out Why

My laptop was stolen
to teach me again
that special joy
when words flow
through a pen.

Here I Raise My Hat

I think that Robert Frost is truly a great poet,
and maybe that's because
he writes as though he didn't know it.

Going Walkies

Now that I must leave
this much-loved place,
my mind is dragging on its lead,
and fighting for each lamp-post
that I leave behind.

And thus I bark and whine
along this path,
where I create my time,
as though I were
a guide-dog who has chosen
to act blind.

Exiles Who've Never Left Home

Their house is small,
and simple, like a home
a child might draw,
but tiles are loose, and walls are cracked,
where roots have pushed beneath the floor.

Each time that I walk by,
I find them, sitting on the rocks
each side the door,
with smiles, so deep
they seem to share
the wonder and the peace
that every life, before its end,
would want to meet.

My reticence holds back
my urge to kneel
before their feet, or even speak,
for I've no words,
that dare disturb
this emptiness
where everything already is
just what it is,
and has no need for more.

Instead, my mind unfolds
the flesh and bone,
that hide my heart,
and holds it out, for them to share,
knowing by their side
it will be safe, till journey's end,
and hoping they'll agree
to keep it there.

Rishikesh: Monsoon Poems

Lofty Amputations

The Ganga's icy waters breathe a mist
that makes it seem I walk in clouds,
threading my way across the Laxman bridge,
among the feet-less crowds.

Haiku, (Plus Optional Words)

Like a stream [that sings] outside my door
the sound of the rain
awakes me, smiling.

Zoological Observation

Why do cows look so sad
in the rain?
With all that hair and hide
you'd think
they'd be glad
to get out of the heat
and have a drink!

I know if I were of their ilk
I'd want to cool my milk.

Rainy Weather

I could sit and read my book all day,
but life sticks in his head, and shouts,
"Come out and play!"

Sartorial Discomfort

Whether humidity comes from the skies,
or from my skin,
my t-shirt's damn uncomfortable
to keep my body in.

Side Effects of Religion

Now it's Guru Poornima
and people come in crowds,
to sing their tributes, loud
and often flat,
to gurus,
who are humbly proud
and often run to fat.

Indian Decibels

VIPs are amplified
to spread
their precious words about.
While less important persons
tend to shout

Paradoxes Transcend Time

It's strange,
that now I am sixty,
I see these serious,
younger men,
still with an eye,
that wonders if I
will one day grow up
to be like them.

Invisible Blues

The one aspect of aging
I rather would have missed
is when the girls look through me
as if I don't exist

Where The Eyes May Lie

I am a fool: unsafe and loud,
when faced by loveliness,
whose shine creates
these shadows,
which appear to be
the x-rays of the horrid side of me.

If it were possible, I'd hide
behind a mask,
which has no holes for eyes,
because it's so much safer
when there is no-one to see.

But here outside, I laugh
at these dramatic thoughts that wed
these visions
of an overactive head.

For all the time
the me, that chose these rôles
is seen, by I,
who merely moves about
so deeply touched by all it finds
that no words need come out.

Problem Of Startling Dimensions

If you want to get somewhere fast, just pray
that no Punjabi family   e - x - t - e - n - d - s   your way.
For everywhere you want to go,
they'll somehow ######## b l o c k ######### entire streets
and jam them to a stop......
or [[*squeeze*]] them so they move dead slow.

Inner Secret Of Buffoon

So prone to misbehave,
and then perhaps regret:
the clown in me: the loud,
attention-seeking clown,
has so much egg across his face,
that he can only smile,
as others turn their backs
on such disgrace.

For though his face has played
its part in many hells,
there is a path straight through the eyes
to where an angel dwells.

How Snaps Can Crackle And Pop

The photos that reveal the truth
are those distorted
by a lack of focus
or a trick of light,
for life has so arranged things
that it's rare to ever find it
wholly sharp and bright.

And thus
the greatest photos speak,
unique as any art,
that blends the visions of the eye
with brushstrokes from the heart.

Still Trying To Figure It Out

My memory is such
that I only wake up
to what I'm not doing,
just as the moments touch.

Riding Away From
The Vultures' Café

I saw two vultures dining
on the carcass of a cow.
My eyes were snatched
by feathers, black and white,
in ragged coats, from which
their baldy heads and bendy necks
would glare and poke.

I could have watched for hours,
but they didn't like
the purring of my motor-bike,
and so they toddled off
behind some rocks, to hide
until they heard me drive away;
thinking in their innocence that I
was not the kind of beast
to lick his lips and steal their feast.

It is, of course, not hard to tell
they didn't know me very well.

Mana 15th July 2006

The Body I Cannot Control

The accidents that threatened me
all yesterday, continued into morning:
so my leg, that managed to survive
being twisted underneath my bike,
when it slipped sideways on the gravel,
found a way to trap itself again:

this time inside the squatter loo,
when it went skidding off
the standing place,
which iced up overnight,
and left my foot
half-stuck inside,
thank God, before the poo!

It seems my right leg craves
a sprain, or break,
and if it tries again, might easily succeed,
however much I try to keep
its ankle in my mind.

It's wobbling now, so wayward
to control, that here,
among the sliding rocks and mud,
it seems I might as well be blind.

The Pleasure Of Not Turning Back

Maybe this low-hanging cloud
is going to stick around all day.
Maybe I should pack my bags
and ride my bike away.

But on the other hand,
it's good to take a stroll
in this unknown space,
where strands of mist
can kiss my face,
until the time arrives
for breeze to blow aside
this veil, that denies to me
the passage of my eyes.

For if I spend all day
in stumbling up through rocks,
yet never see the view,
the close relationship I find
with tiny flowers, and scents,
that only rise inside a mist,
is company enough.

And though the mind may grumble
at its blindness to the sights,
the senses of my body
have been touched.

For, even in the dimness of this light,
a colour and a freshness tremble,
deep and sweet, within
the emptiness, that lies
beneath my skin.

Rise & Shine

At last the clouds begin to shift.
It seems the sun has had enough
of sleeping on his eiderdown,
and feels ready now to set his feet
back on the ground.

A True Reward For Public Service

The Tehri Dam is finished now
and waiting for a VIP to find the time
to come around
and close its doors.
Let's hope that he will also be
the first to drown
when nature quakes and roars.

Flickers Of The Past

Watching bits of Hindi flicks,
in chai-shop black and white,
can bring an unexpected joy,
when eyes accept whatever
is delivered to their sight.

Gwaldam 18th July 2006

The poems in this book mainly arise in that space where mind is free of problems. But freedom cannot sit complacently on fear and sorrow and sometimes their voices must be heard.

It happened in this small mountain town, where nightfall brought me to a stop after a day of pot-holed, narrow roads, that threw me about, slowed me down and knocked me breathless with the beauty of the land.

The next morning, as I wandered around, these words insisted on being heard, so I sat on a rock and started to write:

Words That Are Hard To Say

Today, I am impotent,
and this is not at all
like "being gay",
for impotence cannot
parade in "pride"
for those who have it
always wish that it
would up, and go away.

It is this hope for change,
and fear that after this
nobody whom I love,
will want to stay,
that makes me so afraid
to share my bed.

For when that moment comes
which others long for,
I am half in love
and more than half in dread.

Words That Grow Easier To Say

When sex has proved impossible,
There is no way, that one
can ever truly say, that it's OK.
But now that I am old enough
and strong enough inside,
to speak these words, despite this shame
that still assaults me as I write,
I will no longer hide;
nor will I blush and carry blame.

I have been made like this,
and though it seems I am denied
my share of bliss,
this trouble has evicted me
to other tracks
where I have found
an independent joy
that I could never dream of
at that time when I
first faced this test
to prove that I was every bit
as good as all the rest.

Yet now, I look at other men and know
their sufferings in other ways
have been as deep as mine.
But there are few who'd have the guts to stand,
as I do now, and say that I am different,
and have been since the day
that I was born;
although it is a truth
that every man might say.

I spit upon that fear that bids me hide
my beauty and my joy in shame,
but Impotence retains
a cruelty, which gouges me,
each time I speak its name

New Verses *(added Sept.2006):*

But now I have to add
that since I've shown these words to other eyes,
and even dared to read them loud
before an audience
I feel a strength and pride,
as though I were a boxer
who has lost his bout,
but gone for fifteen rounds,
without being counted out.

So now I do not flinch and turn away,
whatever light is thrown on my face.
For there is nothing there
that is not worthy of embrace.

Full House

The hand that I've been dealt is meant for me,
and though I did not choose the cards today,
there seems a choice that's mine:
whether to weep and chuck them in,
or pick them up and play.

Kausani 19-20*th* July 2006

Eyeing The Forbidden Fruit

Naspati are light green fruits,
that are uneven in their shape,
somewhere between a boulder and a pear,
and often big as fists and just as hard:
for should you get their skin between your teeth,
it takes a mighty heaving on the toothpick
to relieve them of this thing like hippo hide,
so tough, that afterwards you find
your teeth are shoved a fraction more apart.

Therefore the wise man, wishing to enjoy
the crunchy, juicy, white within,
will first employ a knife, to help it shed its skin.

And thus, I would enjoy to eat
this glistening, refreshing treat,
but am denied; for though each tree
that stands before me now
is laden down with fruit,
and it is rotting, wormy by the roads,
it is impossible to buy, except in 40 kilo sacks
that I can't carry on my back,
so there is nothing left
to do, except to climb the fence
and try a little theft.

Helping Me On "The Way"

"Where have you been?
Just look at your self!
Who do you think you are?"
my mother asked.

And thus she was the Guru
who first set me on this path.

Something To Chuang Tzu On

Does tongue taste tea,
or is it nose?
Or does the tea taste me?
Nobody knows.

This non-duali-tea
is far more subtle in its taste
than one may first suppose.

The Gourmet's Treat

There are many grades of tea
and I would like to try each one:
to feel the different grades of me
with each taste on my tongue.

Neighbours Not Chosen, But Planted

The tea plants of Kausani
have no voices like
the maize plants of McCleod.

But they are orthodox you see
(at least it says so on the box),
and this amazing view
of high and mighty peaks
may breed a little snobbery,
and so perhaps they do not speak to me.

For I am of the crowd, not highly born,
and anyone who spends his time
in gossiping with corn,
is probably beneath their scorn.

Looking About

I am so much blest,
what more could I desire,
since there is no lower
and no higher?

Exactly Where Do I Find My Ear?

Here in this fog
there is such silence,
one can hear
an underlying sound,
behind the bird calls
and the motor
of a solitary truck.

Is it the voice of trees and grass
conversing with the fog?
Is it the hum of distant
streams and cars?

Or could it be
the energy of life itself
that speaks to me?

Foggy Morning Meditation

I am alone forever.
Therefore here is where the peace
will have to be:
that peace, which goes beyond the usual ends
of sharing the approval and the love,
that may be found, with family and friends.

The cord that bore my food and blood
was cut when I was born,
but when it comes to mental strings,
that cutting did not change a thing:
I was, and am, alone.

But this is plain ridiculous,
for body only is
when senses tell the eyes and flesh,
with all its other sensual holes,
that they exist.

And yet despite being touched
from every side, this voice goes on
that cries, "I am alone."

Alone from what?
To be alone there has to be some frame
that makes an inside and an out,
where other things exist,
and show their backs to give
a meaning to the word.

And since the body cannot be
without being touched
by air or solid things
it must be something else
that feels the vacancy
which makes this lonely me.

Perhaps it has to do
with talking to myself:
this voice that says,
"I want a bit of this,
but less of that.
I want to be defined,
and only know myself
in seeing some reflection
in a mind that is not mine,"
in hope I'll fall in love
with these reflections that I find.

But in more usual times
I know that I detest
the loathing or indifference
that seems to turn its back on me
and leaves again this loneliness
to fill up all I see.

I am alone, as I perceive the trees
approaching through the fog,
and tiny ants that stroll
around my table top
to feed on biscuit crumbs,
and see the hand
which holds this pen
and sense this thought
which still insists: I am alone.

There is a craziness in this
which has the power
to bring enormous joy.
For who is it who sees all this
but one who only can exist
if not alone,
because he sees all this.

And who is it that feels
this one is there,
but one who never has been born,
who knows
there never has been one to be alone.

Holy Grail

Always half full and half empty my cup:
a miracle it stays that way,
even though I slake my thirst
every moment of the day!

Catch 21.9

The bucket of hot water's free,
but where's the room-boy
I must ask to bring it me?

Making Mean Faces

When I complain, the anger,
so sincere, is shallower than lipstick
on the mouth of this deep fear
that I have been found out,
and all can see the insignificance
of me, that trembles in the clothes I wear.

That's why I cannot bear my indignation,
even as I fume about the lack of service,
in the face of he, who has the gall
to say he was too far away
to hear the yells of my repeated call.

It may be true. Indeed
he could have been pre-occupied
with jobs that kept him
from me, when I felt this need
to fill my stomach and my time.
But he is paid to serve me
so I have the right to whine.

And so I spill my misery
across his life, which he must take
without complaint, but as he walks away
perhaps his anger dwells
on how a mouth can be
a garbage-chute, and mind
a place for constipated swine.

And thus I see that his ideas of me
have now become the same as mine.

Malignant Humours

I'm good at resentments,
but tend to drop them fast,
once they have been well-expressed.

The problem is to start
to get them off my chest.

Suspect Presents From The Present

The promises that life has made
are very rarely kept.
And that is why it surely pays
never to expect

On Losing Choosing

The unexpected
is that
which cannot be rejected,

and thus:

"the best laid schemes of mice and men"
are turned upon their heads again.

.

The Joy Of Counselling Couples

Are my poems growing
less sophisticated?

Perhaps it's just the words
that knock upon my mind,
then walk in, hand in hand,
already mated.

Chucking Down The Gauntlet

For those who write
the standard stuff of poetry:
that image feast
where you can eat
and then, as quick, forget;
my threadbare words
may seem a little trite.

So please excuse my cheek
that it's ideas
I choose to speak,
and though they may lack paint
they do contain some meat.

And maybe something more,
that may remain,
when all the clever images
are swallowed by the drain.

To One, Whose Words Speak More Than Their Sum

Anjali, these pictures
that you knock together
from the sound,
and shape of words,
have thrown me in so deep,
that lost and whirl-pooled
are my feet, that can
no longer find some ground
on which to stand.

The place that you convey
is far too much alive
for any photograph to speak,
and mind, that can't conceive,
is staggered back,
a long way from the edge,
where it can only dare
to wriggle on its tum,
a long safe distance from
this moment, which
it has no means to share.

But there is that inside
which feels, where no interpreter
has been, that is so satisfied,
that nothing need be understood.

And wild words can bang together
to make shapes no eyes have seen,
that come and go so fast,
that they remain ungrasped,
although there never was a moment
when they have not been.

I hesitated before including this next poem, but it stays, because it reflects the tragic news I heard from Gaza and the West Bank, day after day.

On Those Who Disgrace Their Race

Because my father was a Jew
I cannot help but feel the disgrace
when little Arab boys and girls
are murdered as they play
because their land is wanted
for The Chosen Race.

Etiquette Cannot Be Taught To Thought

Thoughts are not polite.
They never knock upon my door
before they wander in.
They suddenly appear
to pick their nose and leer
or hog the fire, as they fill
my easiest armchair.

I do not care to share the place
with such unruly louts, but when
I have evicted them,
I find myself outside the door
without the key
to readmit me to my room.

And then it slowly comes to me
that when all thoughts are gone
no room can be.

And then "*what*" slowly comes to "*who*"?
becomes my thought,
thus trapping me again in that
which a thought has brought.

Paparsali, Almora 24th July 2006

Postcard Piece

Yesterday I did not write,
but now I have my pen in hand,
as I look out, across
the many shapes and stands
of pines and deodars,
until they are so far away
that they appear
no bigger than the bristles
on the dark upended chins
of distant hills, that stand
where valley clouds
are brushed across in strands.

While up above them, where the sky
is wholly grey, I try
to calculate how high will be
the jagged Himalayan heads,
beneath their snowy sheets,
if wind will move
these clouds aside,
to show the giant wonders,
sleeping, deep and vast, inside.

Choosing The Cards To Discard

It's strange: the friends I came to see
revealed no sign of heart to me.
It was the ones I'd never met before
that made me glad I'd braved
my shyness and my fear,
to knock upon this door.

Giving Away The Piggy-Bank

Surrender means
the ending of the known.
No more boxes; no more keys;
no safety nets, no certainties.

For where no feet have trod
my feet must walk,
and yet I feel no fear,
for I am sure
each step will fall
exactly in the place,
that is uniquely made
to hold my sole
in its embrace.

Tossing The Coin With No Sides

The voice that says that this is me
has rarely ceased to speak
while I have been awake;
but this that is not me, yet is,
has never had a voice
but always is,
and which I am this moment
seems beyond my choice.

Pedigree Chum

The mind can be a hound,
that barks and sniffs
at its own scent,
as it suspects
the owner of its thoughts
of hypocritical intent.

But, as I gravely wonder
what this state might mean, I see
my mind is rushing round
with tail in its mouth.
And then it is not hard
to drop my frown,
and laugh so much,
I have to find a tree.

*Being born in The Year of the Dog
suggests that there may be
validity
for those who would describe me as
an s.o.b*

Crystal Balls Are Misty

Will it be simplicity
and laughter that I find,
when I go visiting today,
or will the complications
that are life, entwine
my heart and mind?

In any case, it's clear
that what this day has sent for me
is going to appear.

And so, beneath the Christmas tree
the present lies, which I approach
with leaping heart,
as fingers fumble
to untie the string.

And I can only guess
at what surprises
have been wrapped within.

Blessings On Their Perceptive Minds

My ego took a leap into the wild
when Meena said
that I was like a child.
Such joy was in my heart,
as when my old friend, Hans,
looked keenly at me and announced,
"Something has changed."
And all I could do was laugh and laugh.

The Value Of Contrast

Now, it's in such joy, this me,
that yesterday was tired out
and glaring at each face
that dared intrude into its space.

It does seem strange
this me should think itself the same
as that which snarled
with such rejection at the minds
which butted in to ask
the same old nosy questions
without caring,
what they'd find

And yet I do not think,
this morning, with its air
that pours inside me, like champagne,
is of a higher birth
than those same nasty times,
that had to be,
to give me some comparison,
to know its worth.

Red-Faced Sahib Ungrunts

Last night such cacophony,
tonight so peaceful,
makes me realise
that when annoyed, by noise,
I turn real beastful

Two Poems on the Effects of Catharsis on Arses

One feels so much better
when shit has been released.
And thus an empty gut can be
more happy than a feast.

....

Once the shit is out,
it rarely hits the fan.
It's when it's stuck inside,
that it destroys a man.

When Skies Descend

It would be mad to go outside
and drench myself in rain,
When nothing really pushes me to leave
this chair, where I can hear
the easy music of the falling drops.

They splash before
this terrace where I sit,
amazed by transformations
wrought by mist
to trees in crowds,
now shoving through the clouds,
to clamber up to crags,
where heaven pours
its new washed hair,
to touch the floor.

Nainital (28th July 2006)

Wonderful mix of corrugated bing-
bong structures, leaning
and creaking themselves, in gaps between
the glossy paint and tinted glass,
of those with new-found wealth,
who shudder from the ancient,
pigeon-roosting remnants of the Raj:
those Hindu-Gothic flying buttresses,
all curlicued with other bits
that sharply elbow neo-classical facades,
among the dubious dives and drives,
all cluttered up with lawyers' signs.

The more commercial streets combine
the cafés of the smart,
that cater for the new elite,
with holes in walls, that offer
momos*, roasting maize, and most of all,
the eggs, that everywhere
are boiled by the poorest of the self-employed,
who hope to rise from rags
to rupees from a bit of ground,
with barely space to turn a rat around.

The whole shebang is perched
along the lower slopes, like tops of feet,
all side by side, that dip their toes
in water, where reflections meet;
and as the eye ascends the woody trouser legs
and skirts, it must eventually arrive
at jagged heads, where picnic parties
once would thrive, after the pleasant ride
through all the mist-fed, rustling green

*'Momos' are a Tibetan form of dim sum.

to lofty haunts, where they could see
the snowy polls of Himalayas,
rising from their beds as if surprised
to stare at us from far beyond
those ranges which intrude with bristly backs
beneath their distant eyes.

But now my sight, which reaches out,
falls short, however hard it tries,
and there is little chance
that they'll come out and take a bow,
for clouds are rushing up the bowl sides
of these crags and spilling off the tops,
like vapours in some chemical experiment,
which overflow the sides of a burette.

And though they're cold and wet, they bless
me as they drive away all but a few
of that vast crowd of bureaucrats,
and business men, with their substantial wives,
and screaming kids, who rush to this retreat,
when holidays from school arrive
and Delhi is a furnace on full heat.

So now it's mainly locals that I meet,
as I go by the jostling storefronts, which compete
to grab my eyes and pockets,
passing by the hungry groups
of tough Nepali porters, small and dark,
with shiny muscles bulging from their calves,
who stand beside the hiring place,
close to the commercial eyes
that have replaced the joy,
that once would shine, from each Tibetan face.

Two football teams, in real colours, draw
a crowd who commentate
with new-found, World Cup expertise,
and eye the local Beckhams, as they chase
across this space, which lies
beside the ornate mosque, all white and green,
in flattering designs, intended to impress
the faithful and the faithless,
as they pray, or scheme

The ball is kicked outside,
and with it go my eyes,
to glide in peace across the lake,
until they meet its other side,
where wavelets lap the promenade
and hotels, not quite grand
stand side by side, transplanted
out of Eastbourne, to this land.

They've travelled far, and higher
than the voices of the choir
of lady Methodists, who once
ascended from the heat,
like thermals rising from the plains,
to take their 'leave' among these high,
but not so 'dark, satanic hills'.

It is not hard to find a lake,
but this one came 'port out,' on P & O*
with cabin trunks brim-full
of dark and slurping waves,
as deep as skies that lower
over fells and pikes,
with heads half-hidden
by the rarely-ending rain,

---

*'Port-Out' + 'Starboard Home' = POSH: the best accommodation on the P & O steamers, which connected Britain to its Indian Empire.

And here it lingers,
exiled from the peaks of home;
although their shades
still haunt the waves,
where lean and hungry boatmen
take their fee, to navigate
the over-weight, excited
families, of would-be VIPs,
whose mobile phones record
their camera pose,
with fifteen seconds
of excited shrieks,
that linger briefly in the mist
which hangs above the deep.

While all around,
the living and the dead,
that make this town,
are too much here, to sleep.

Dawn

This is the time when the unspoken
gropes for words,
before the crash and bang
of thought-roads stuffs me up
like some old gossip
leaning on the fence
to natter at the air.

This is the time for me to be inside:
indeed my reading specs
unfocus anything that lies
beyond a yard away;
but here, in emptiness, within,
resides a spinner, who can make
of nothing: everything.

With No Specks On My Specs

All it takes is open eyes,
and then I walk
through paradise.

Looking Back Before I'm Gone

Each moment is created by the mind,
and in this leaving time
its elbows grow more pushy,
as they shove aside
the easy joy of Now,
to turn the heart
and stretch it in reverse,
to that idyllic time
that must be left behind.

And when the mind
yearns back like this,
to drag my eyes away
from all the rare
revealings of this day,
that wait for me
with beating heart to find,
it is my choice, alone,
to walk with backward feet
this way of hurt,
so I may feel
the bruises of the blind.

Visionary Substance

Dripping mist is different from rain.
It is an essence you can breathe,
that bares the scents and colours
of the flowers and leaves,
so easily unnoticed in the brazen light,
that moves the eye to places not so close
as these: that cluster round my feet, and leave
wet traces of their touch,
on trouser legs and sleeves.

The mist has often
been a veil for myth.
It is a gate in time,
through which, maybe, a dragon waits,
or long-lost legions clatter by,
to vanish round the bend,
where dripping ferns become mixed up with sky;
and so do I.

Chitrakut 1ˢᵗ August 2006

On Not Discussing Where To Put The Change

A totally naked bloke
is wandering round in this town,
and he is so at ease
as he sits down to sip his tea,
beside his mates,
all clothed in normal gear,
it makes me wonder why
I am so shy to be like him and leave
my underwear behind,
when I feel like a chai.

Afterthought On Recent Lines

Sometimes these poems seem
to leap from toe to toe,
and since the path ran out
and slammed the door,
I'm not at all surprised:
for how else would they go?

Just Call Me Tate, Mate

I am my own art gallery.
Each room obeys the golden rule
so perfectly
that walls have never met
the ceiling or the floor,
and thus there is no need
to tire out my feet
as I explore.

Hearing When You're Not Here

Though all ears seem open
there's another secret door
that opens with the kick of noise
and says, "Hello, I hear!"
But shuts itself again
to simple sounds
which do not break
this silence which
the simple sounds do make.
And when such sounds are heard,
there is no me,
to tell me I'm awake.

Tiruvannamalai 12-24th August 2006.

Waiting, *at the end of my ride, were many official documents from banks and agencies, but only one letter that was written from a friend. It was unmistakably hers, scrawled beautifully in its ink, statuesque and bold. Reading it, this poem arose in response:*

Real Friends Have No Ends

Heather, I see you there,
with your big, pale face, emerging from all
the woollies of your jumper,
with the heavy skirt and stripy socks,
that stick out underneath;
a giant mug of tea in hand,
or maybe plate of thick-cut bread,
well spread, with all the goodies
that a tum deserves,
to compensate for all the aches and pains
each day throws up.

I see you sitting there,
much bigger than life-size, and hard to move
as Henry Moores, that stretch in comfy gardens,
with a view of flowers through the holes,
that let the breezes through.
But you are made of other stuff
than bronze or granite,
that has never known the beat of heart,
or rush of blood, which are so much of you.

As you sit there, between the arms
of your big chair, still safe and yet unsafe,
although you seem protected from the storm,
there is a glinting in your eyes
and miles and miles of life,
still turbulent and brimming,
in each atom of your great big, woolly form.

The Clock's Alarm Cannot Harm

As soon as eyes are open,
mind pants up,
all creased and hustly,
in its race to fill my day
with those decisions I must make,
on all the things I have to do,
now I'm awake.

But life will do them anyway
and use me now and then,
if I turn out to be
its nearest tool.

So I am free to smile
at these thoughts,
which grab this space
but then rush off so fast.

For those with such a short-term lease
can make their moonlit flits in peace.

The Sound of Two Ears Waggling

Spiritual progress cannot be,
since one is either deluded or free.
And since the delusion is you and me,
how can spiritual progress be?

What Is Before And After

I have no words to speak it,
and, without words
can thinking be?
How can it express itself
except as this?
And who or what am I,
this witness,
who can never know
just what it seems to see,
except my Self,
so undefined and free,
that nothing, really nothing
needs to be.

How The Future Becomes Present

"The World is totally full
of unfinished business.

When will it end?"

"The World, or the unfinished business,
my friend?"

Worlds can come and go,
but unfinished business
never ends.

The Point Of The Book

I guess I love to rave about
my spiritual affairs,
but still I have to ask myself,
"Who cares?"

The End Of The Road

To go where none
has gone before
sounds great,

But, to arrive and find
nobody there,
can lead to sadness
one should contemplate,
when stepping out alone
to meet with fate.

But on the other hand,
a look into alone may show
that nobody has come, or gone,
or been alone, to know.

Part II

Some Moments From Different Indian Voyages
(Quietly thieved from my other books)

Silent Night, Holy Night? *2010*

Night has no silence.
It is full of clangs
and starting engines.

Even here,
so many miles out of town,
there is a constant
chirp of insects,
or the fall of rain
explodes the throats
of frogs, who kettle drum
and croak,
more noisy than the stars.

And now, tonight,
the sound of inspiration,
in my head, has opened up my eyes,
to stare alarmed at where the fingers
of my clock
have barely crawled
past 3 a.m

A brightness from the sky
is peering underneath
my curtain
to inform me
that the moon
is just about to leave,
and as I stagger forth
to hurl the pee
out of its jug, I see

a shooting star
burn up its tail.
So what a hope has sleep?

With nights so full of life,
they make my heart
all full of beat!

Indian Child *2008*

This face that shines
before me, on the street,
is so wide open
there is nothing
left to meet.

Song From A Minaret *1967*

Allah, in your eyes I am more naked
than the space between the stars.
Your hand is like a cloak of wool
as I stand trembling on the mountainside.
Your lips pour songs of skylarks
to my soul.

You fill my skin
with radiance and I am nothing
but a space within your skies
through which you shine as wine
that pours with moonlight in its eyes.

Holy Neighbours *1980s*

Here, holy men attract
more dreams than pop stars.
All night long the buses come,
disgorging fans who crowd
in hustling lines to touch
the maharishi's feet,
and chant his name,
at least, until the dawn.

And all the night
his name in neon lights competes
with other stars
more silent and more deep,
that still excite me every time
I crawl out from my bed,
disturbed by all the noise
to take a pee,
and then, (thank God),
go back to sleep.

What is Masochism? *1968*

Life without a moon
shining on temples
like this.

Secret Rendezvous *1968*

I tiptoe before the moon.
My secret is the dawn:
flowers and colours
all uncrumpling
after a good night's sleep.

On The Swami's Birthday   1978
(remembering Sri Annamalai Swami)

Feasting finished;
now, the violence
of music, twisted
in the gross exhaling
of distorted speakers
gone .... at last ...

They wander through the trees
beside the pond,
and exercise their bellies
as they beat
their threadbare clothes,
eroding rocks,
as dust of days
is washed away,
or once again
is given to the skies.

The chatter of their voices,
matched by songs of birds,
seems sweeter now ...

But through all this
the holy man they celebrate,
unmoved,
has borne the love and praise
they sing before his face.

He comes now, solitary,
passing through the trees:
the sun, in silence,
throwing light upon the leaves .

Drought *1968*

Because there is no water,
tonight we shall wash with stars
and breathe the fragrance
of our skin and hair.

Thirst *1968*

A flower dying in pain,
praying for thunder.
gasping for rain.

Skyholed *1970s*

Now surprised by storm,
amazing and most blessèd:
heaven, heavy cloud mass,
slow as sleepless pillow,
moving merciless against the breath,
itself, is slashed
and scattered to a burst
of light: great hole in sky,
and universe beyond
all fire, shouting.

Even dried up seeds
of centuries untwist to life,
and man, as small as he may be,
grows huge as chestfulls,
towers like balloon,
as lightning slashes
through the ropes,
he flies.

Poem In Two Movements   *1975*
(After the Pushkar Brahmin spoke of
 the dancing peacocks and everything)

It is raining in the forest;
peacocks now are dancing
where the trees are drinking colours
till they burst their flowers open
to the heavens, sweet with water.

....

The sage,
seeing this illusion,
turns the page
to a scene of snow and pollution.

But still he sees,
and almost hears
the dance of birds.

Fondling their plumage,
he sighs,
"Those who talk of illusion
carry blindfolds in their words."

Attempting Non-Discrimination *2009*

Garbage piles jostle,
with a range of shapes
and colours, wilder
than roses in a garden
fresh with dew,
which captivate my gaze,
and call myself to sink
inside soft grass,
oblivious to time.

So why the rush,
to hustle by
when I meet, face to face,
this heap of textures,
forms, and colours,
rarely found, where nature,
by itself, has filled
the palette and the brush?

I study it, and try
to sympathise
with all this mass
of crumpled rags
and broken plastic,
basking in the richness
of the rot, of vegetables
and fruit, that's over-ripe,
among the other bits
of our discarded stuff.

But there is nothing here,
to hold my hand, or touch my heart;
so, sadly, I look round
to find a rock, to scrape my shoes
before I part.

On Trying To Stretch A Moment *2009*

The transience of moments is my life.
I never have been more than this
and cannot be.

The suffering is hanging on
and trying to stretch a brittle
second, that can only break
and leave a painful gap

To peer back at this wound and ask
what happened in this flash
that could not last.

To take a dream of hopes
and to pretend that
threading them,
like pearls in ropes,
can somehow make a me.

I have become
a junky for such trips,
and cannot kick them easily,
for where, without these clothes,
could I step out
and feel and see?

Their transience
and their fragility
is all that I
can ever be.

Roadside View *2007*

I'm losing count of saints.
These Hindu gods have got so many heads
that streets are full of them:

A rickshaw-wallah sleeps with body stretched
along the crossbar, just a metre
from the scarred head of the six year old
who wipes the tables where the tourists eat,
while down below,
a widow offers tears at Kali's feet.

Benares *1969*

Here, by Ganga river,
all the hours of the earth
accumulate and fly
away in dust.

A clutch of sadhus
choke the chillum,
smoking out
across the sunset
with the breath
of bones.

The river is soft.
The river is soft.

Ganga *1969*

What fire, at the tired end
of long days of desire?
What fire, when the furnace hammer
has beaten the anvil to dust?

My naked feet place warily
their bruises, on the stones,
and drag my head
towards the sky,
that rages with great shapes,
of burgundy and grey.

On roads all over India,
the buffaloes drift home
under a sky like this.

The sadhu stands,
in silhouette:
his trident, black
before the flames, that tear
great mouthfuls of the sky,
and spit them on the waves.

Unload the shrouds.
The dead are gone:
as roasted flesh
turns into ash,
the hard staff smashes down,
to crack the head.

And spread, upon the water,
night comes on,
as, in the black,
the fires roar
along the shore;
and bones are cracked once more,
as the great clubs fall.

The river is soft.
The river is always soft.
It flows.

That's all.

Kevan Myers...

... was born, and lived a while, in London; then took off, thumbing his way to many lands; and now that planes are cheap, he always bags a window seat, hoping for cloudless skies to show the ground below, where still, his itchy feet have dreams to spread their toes..

In 1967, he set off to round the World, but got waylaid, in Punjab, sitting backwards on a horse-cart, faced by setting sun which spread across the skies, between the trees; accompanied by clopping hooves and birds with wild cries.

He found that India had grabbed his hand and when he dared to think to leave, she wouldn't let him go.

He tried twice more to round the globe, but every time she mugged him on the road, and stole his watch, and spun him round, then dragged him to a holy place, deep in the South, where, by some grace, he found the place to plant some trees and build the house where he would stay, for many years. And even now it still remains his winter refuge, far from the cold and damp of Northern climes.

But other seasons brought a heat that roasted him too much, and at those times, he fled to where the Himalayan peaks look down from high at hilly feet. Then on he went to places, cool and distant, like Alaska, which held him amazed for two summers.
But then, he opted to try out Europe again.

He set off exploring the back roads of France in a motor-home, which carried him one day to an odd-shaped house, with a gorgeous view, on terraces beneath the kind of tower, where Rapunzel dwells, on the edge of a rough-hewn granite village, deep in the forested, Corrèze hills.

And there he now resides most of the year, enjoying his time with new-found friends, helping to inspire and organise the writers' group, where many of these poems first saw life.

Between these times, in other lands, he worked in schools, in Britain and in Denmark, trying to teach the words and tools that make it possible to speak the feelings and the thoughts which make each being unique.

Of course he learnt as much from those he taught as they found out from him. And still their unchanged souls will bring him smiles on frequent visits to his thoughts and dreams.

But other moments may deliver nightmares where he panics in his mind, pursued by time, unable to recall his teaching plans and gather up his stuff, till suddenly he wakes up, half-way to a class, completely in the buff.

He's much relieved that he escaped in time; as governments turned classrooms into prisons, where each move must be pre-planned and given marks, for fear that raging fires might spring from any stray creative sparks.

It's now a long time since he left, with few regrets and now he lives a different life in each of his two homes.

In France he's glad to shower with hot water, park himself in comfy chairs and eat and drink too much.

But India remains the place which feeds his soul, and heals his body from the excess of the West, with simpler food, and ancient cures, which send him back more youthful than he came.

And while he's there you'll find him still, inside or near, the round and simple house, he built, beside the holy mountain, in that climate where his windows never close, and sleeping can take place, high on his roof, near to the breathing trees and stars, which peer through the mosquito net, to light his face.

Other Poetry from Kevan Myers:

The Kiss Of Life (2018)

In paperback, from Amazon.co.uk at https://amzn.to/2O8I4IA
or dancingyeti@gmail.com
As Kindle (mobi) ebook from: Amazon.com: https://amzn.to/2ZKD7qM
Amazon.co.uk: https://amzn.to/2CyEOuX

is (2009)

Salvage From The Ark (1978)

Available from dancingyeti@gmail.com
where contact, thoughts and criticism are welcome.

Facebook page: 'Kevan Myers: poems and thoughts': http://bit.ly/2JQETk1

Websites: kevanmyerspoetry.com, or dancingyetibooks.com

Author's photo, copyright © Jim Lemkin 2018.

www.ingramcontent.com/pod-product-compliance
Lightning Source LLC
Chambersburg PA
CBHW062148100526
44589CB00014B/1745